TARTS
AND
MUGGERS

Poems New and Selected

TARTS AND MUGGERS

Poems New and Selected

SUSAN MUSGRAVE

McClelland and Stewart Limited

The Canadian Publishers
McClelland and Stewart Limited
25 Hollinger Road
Toronto, M4B 3G2

Canadian Cataloguing in Publication Data

Musgrave, Susan, 1951-
    Tarts and muggers : poems new and selected

ISBN 0-7710-6660-0

I. Title.

PS8576.U8T37   C811'.54   C82-094275-8
PR9199.3.M84T37

35,831

For Jeffrey

CONTENTS

ACKNOWLEDGEMENTS

Poems in this book have been selected from the following collections: *Songs of the Sea-Witch* (Sono Nis Press, 1970); *Selected Strawberries and Other Poems* (Sono Nis Press, 1977/second printing, 1980); *The Impstone* (McClelland and Stewart, 1976); *A Man to Marry, A Man to Bury* (McClelland and Stewart, 1979).

Of the new poems included, some have been published or have been accepted for publication in the following magazines and anthologies:

In Australia: *Helix*

In Canada: *Arts Manitoba; Aurora: Canadian Writing 1978; Benchmarks; Canadian Forum; Event; Exile; Prism International; Room of One's Own*

In Mexico: *Semana Bellas Artes*

In the United Kingdom: *Aquarius; Bananas; New Departures; Slow Dancer; Trends*

In the United States: *South Shore*

"Conversation During The Omelette Aux Fines Herbes" was also published as a Sceptre Press pamphlet, in England, 1979. The title is from a poem "Eight For Luncheon" by Cynthia Macdonald.

"Recognition Not Enough" is a line taken from a poem by Stevie Smith.

is poetry. Of a kind, mind you,
and not to suit everybody's taste.

But this is not a poem for just
anybody. No, in fact, it is meant
for my family.

It is a poem to strangers, then,
on the occasion of Christmas. We sit
sipping smart cocktails, funereal almost
in our elaborate decoration. Around us the room
is dangerously lit.

Every year it is the same ritual –
it sounds quite normal I know and I
suppose it is. *Smile, smile.* I unwrap
each gift with the same cautious enthusiasm
in which it was no doubt chosen.
My young brothers twitch and their
tinselly wives twitter. My mother laughs too
in spite of my own happiness.
Even my father the undertaker is smiling to himself
as he opens another box and quietly closes it again.

THE EXECUTIONER'S CHRISTMAS

The dead are forecasting
bad weather.
When they called me
out of my sleep
I wanted to tell you
"They aren't really there"
but you had gone away again
after some other kill.

I drew myself
all around me. I couldn't escape
don't you see,
so don't ask me
to come with you anymore.
The dead
turn their eyes down,
their heartbeats lessen.
They might scream,
"IS THIS ALL!"
and I would have to tell them
– yes.

I followed you
down into the orchard
frightened because I heard their voices
and smelled the blood in the fire
as I drew too near.
I wanted you
whole
as you once were
but when I was finished
all I could find
was a knife, a few small bones

and you
with your black, black wings.

VAMPIRES SHOULD BE LIBERATED

I think
vampires should be
liberated –
tended like
war memorials.
As a group they should win
the Nobel Prize for
peace.

Nobody likes
failures –
it's all right to
die but don't
disappoint anyone.
It's easy to laugh –
vasectomies make sense
after all.

Equal rights
for vampires –
slave-labour must
end. Free blood
for nursing
mothers, compulsory
dental care.

Relax.
It's simple.
Dying is a free
experience –
enjoy.
If the teeth fit,
bite it. Ignore the
politicians – they're bound
to take death
seriously.

DUE PROCESS

After an article by Ben Metcalfe

So there was this
small celebration in the
prison kitchen afterwards,
with doughnuts and
well-laced coffee and
idle talk of the last
double-noose ceremony.

One of the boys took seventeen minutes
to die. The other,
twenty-three. They fell together
without a sound
though you could see from their eyes
they had been weeping recently.

They say a good hangman
is hard to find;
a good man is even harder.

Hobbled out, prayed over
trussed bagged noosed and dropped

strangulation completes the process
sooner or later.

THE HOUSE AND THE GARDEN

These days are treacherous –
like cut vines and murderous roots
the flowers in the garden
grow deliberately out of proportion.
Insensitive, they are colourless
and don't leave any room for the grass.

Trees uproot themselves
sending hidden fingers
to hide the sun.

The stones are automatically bored.

When I walk outside
devils sit and guard the rabbit holes.
The fence is indifferent
and the vegetables never get
enthusiastic about anything.

I've given up simply trying
to understand. Small animals mate
between the walls of my house.
I'm afraid it too will soon
disappear – most of my neighbours
wish I would leave.

Because of them
there hasn't been any weather
for over a year.

I am such a sad young girl
and they are such horrible old men.

I met a dead man walking in the woods today,
myself a healthy woman, barely twenty-seven.
His breath smelled of white wine and wild
strawberries – the finest white wine and the
ripest fruit.

It was intoxicating.
Our dogs gambolled together,
one black and the other white.
I told him the story of my whole life,
as far back, that is, as I chose to remember.
He wanted to know if I would be his wife –
I said under the circumstances
that would be impossible.

We reached the road that led to my house –
he kissed me, very gently.
He wanted to take me all the way,
after another kiss I agreed and invited him in
for a small meal and some light music.

One kiss more and I was on the floor
when who should walk in but my husband,
a horticulturist.
He had a cauliflower from the garden
he wanted to show me but when he saw us lying there
he said your dog is in the garbage
fighting with another dog

I just thought I'd mention it.

My dead man revived quite quickly,
aroused by being caught in such a compromising position.
I assured him my husband abhorred all forms of violence
and poured us each a stiff drink in the drawing room.

"Your wife tells me you enjoy gardening,"
our guest says, as I slip off into the kitchen to make
a good cheese sauce for my husband's cauliflower.
Small talk has never interested me
particularly.

"O GRAVE WHERE IS THY VICTORY"

I Corinthians 15:55

Yesterday
I loved you
today well
I don't know
death never
hesitates
death wants to
get married.
Death does not
eat properly
death believes in
civilization
death drinks
beer
death watches
hockey
death is
invincible
death is always
happy.
Yesterday I
loved you
well today I don't
know
death has
false teeth
death has
bad habits
death makes me
furious
death is
possessive
germs feed on
death but

death doesn't
know that.
Yesterday
well I think
I loved you
but now I
just don't know
death wants me
to live with him
death would make life
impossible
death wants to
meet my family
death wants
babies
death believes
true love is
eternal
death depends on things being
finished.
I don't think
death knows himself
death is,
after all,
only human.

COMING OF AGE

The pit at midnight
crusty with snow
like day-old bread pudding

and Giffey the outlaw
giving a sermon about sin

right down there
in a preacher's black gown

only his cock and his
cloven hoof peeping out a little.

The chalk pit where
Giffey would show us his stump.
We used to line up for him,
undaunted by his obscene gestures.

And show him *our* proud bodies.

All nine of us, nubile and
cheeky, dancing just out of his
reach

and old Giffey getting all creamy
and churned up
with each of us worrying and wriggling
like that.

We were so quick
we teased him until he came,
blasting off into the moonlight
for all the world to watch.

Then he would cry
and we thought he was crazy,
not daring to come close or
touch, not near enough for
comfort.

We were the peaty source of his
darkness, with our lies and our smiles
and stories about our lives.
For there were no blessings in our cold
eyes, only cruelty, and more of that for
our youth.

At night I would dream of
giving myself to him,
being drilled into the dirt,
cursing and carrying on like
old Giffey himself when his
wormy thing wouldn't get hard.

I saw myself kneeling below him,
opening myself before him,
lying open beneath him

tightening and tempting

until one night he never
came anymore.

We were haunted and stripped
naked at last, eager for
whatever unpleasantness he would
permit

anxious for all his ungainliness:

he never came.

Colder than ever in that chalk
pit tracing circles with our toes

we crept home finally to our
clean beds, long past the usual
hour, completed and alone.

THE SPILLED CHILD

Now, too,
you are wanting
the spilled child out of me,
the last part
unbroken down
    – the abandoned bird
      wingless and screaming
      in a corner –

Now you too.
Down among the many dawns
bleached in iron rivers
whoring on chains
of muddy fish –
            you too
in the blackness that bites off
all the white flowers,
the darkness that meets you
everywhere
with sad news from home –
            you too
want the spilled child
to die in secret
or not at all,
to sew her body
to the ground with worms
or preen all the birds' songs
of waiting
    – the birds that drag the night
      like a black sheet
      in their beaks –

while our hearts and kidneys
crash like cymbals
   – some of them were
     torn into pieces
     because of their refusal to sing –

So I will go
and in the black spring
I will pick dead flowers.
At night I will overturn stones.
Curious and broken
the spilled child
will burn
reluctantly and for a long time.

THE CHILD BRIDE

After a while I shall learn
that disappointment seizes
the worst of all my gains –
anything else becomes a
better prospect. It is quite
insulting to be vague and
full of love – as if I couldn't
live without him. Pride is loose
in my blood and then sets in.
One by one
I take all my things away,
wincing on the dark shelf
above the bridegroom
offering peace.

A casual ceremony, no
black goodbyes – no children
begging in the shadows towards alarm.
Where? How? As usual
I am caught
off guard.

This that has crumbled,
this is what I had.
I burned out in expectation,
night fell
earlier, a quick new life
or else, a clear one.
Nothing in between. I couldn't
allow it, not for anybody's sake.
I fell
and scraped my knees
badly – why was I there?

Food for my lover's
child bride. Sullen stain.
And dead sounds,
the reverence of leaving.
Anywhere around
he'd shed me; what is it
that he wants so hard?
Earth alone is indestructible.
I lie in defeat for the years.

Under the snow
and foxes barking,
a skull winked
   - my grandmother saw it -

Snow on the wind
and yard lamps
blinking
   - she could hear her footsteps
     on the unpaved road -

Cold dreams in the night
drilled the wet untired dark
   - in the hour, the season
     she tamed them with her plough -

Ice in the well
and broken windows
   - she would glue together
     the shattered pieces,
     set them in
     like precious stones -

Snow on the hill,
imaginary lane
   - she would die first
     for all the others dying,
     carted away
     thick and blistered

Absent in the dust and
patient in her chair.

AFTER THE RAIN

After the rain
the field-gates open,
the slanting sun
trims our tired wet bones;

we scream the vowels
of freedom,
the wheel tracks freshen
as hell falls through –

by the road
grandpa finds us
unreal mushrooms,
red, brown
and orange –
an unreal grandpa
who knows the calls of all the birds,

who sings and sighs
a snail of the vain and ugliest

while our lips mould the smoke of fallen starlight
and our hearts toll like clappers
in the bell of dark.

A CURIOUS CENTURION

I met him on a mountain
black cowl covering his head
a sniper in the heather he led
me down into the stony pasture

cushioned my heart on a fleshy pillow,
fed me spiced milk on a ruined altar.

He lived on the mountain, he said,
lured holy men and saints to go that way
on pilgrimage. I was lucky to get off
with my life; being a child saved me.

His legions were deserting, delivered
out of the melancholy of armour.
From my damp bed I heard the tramp of the
corpse-carriers; bog-ghosts croaking like
gods unworshipped.

I prayed for him, a devil's dark prayer –
haunted over the bare slopes, hunted
through a dry season. I had a tin drum
and a toy gun, a gambler's wild hand and
a warrior's reason.

War was all around; the deceitful moon
rose with undefeatable custom. She shone
with more cunning than the fusty prophets
of my cursed village. There was always a
war going on. My father had his own gun,
and it was real.

I remember the humming of wild bees,
an old sheep with no eyes, those
far-seeing ravens. I climbed to that
church where the marble deity lay fallen,
a shrine desecrated and unholy.

I remember the shadow on the cross
carried by warm winds over the warm grass

and the song of the soldiers going home
at last

whitethorn in their helmets,
flags of surrender.

CARNIVAL

I only remember the rats,
he said. Nothing else, no,
not even the tired grey women
selling tickets to the
tunnel of love.

Not the bodies of the young girls
blooming like caught sails
under the sky, or monks
in their sensuous robes, fingering
their delicate lutes.

Not even the balloon man with his
spotted dog, nor the drinking
jester, nor the faith-healer
with a little bowl in his hands.

I remember counting the rats.
One night there were eight of them
sharing the shabby bedsit.

They became an obsession.
In the morning when you woke
to face a soft underbelly it was
delectable nostalgia. Weapons
were futile; you pitted yourself
against their skills.

You were a fellow-sufferer.
You found your identity in
wiping them away. For days at a time
you had nothing else to eat.
But even rats cannot stop
dullness creeping in.

I started dreaming of women.
Their split sex seemed an enigma,
monstrous. I had no wish for such
meaningless opulence.

My foraging became inhuman.
I gorged myself nightly beneath
beercellars and dancehalls.
I saw how dangerous my own waste
had become, and social barriers
non-existent.

I only remember the rats.
It was their ruthlessness I admired,
their lack of religion. I took hold of them
in my hands, squeezing life out of them
as gently as you would shake laughter out of
children.

Perhaps *they* were laughing at the
indignities I made them suffer. In the end
their pain was more welcome than a friend.

But their suffering was far more
permanent than my own: when one died
there was always a replacement.

I remember the rats,
he said. Nothing else, no,
only the rats.
Not the tired grey women
selling tickets to the
tunnel of love, not even
the bodies of the young girls.

THE ANGEL-MAKER

"Angel-makers. That's what they
used to call abortionists."

Margaret Laurence, *A Jest of God*

I am old, my horoscope has run out.
My head-dress terrifies you, I know,
but let me assure you one mask only conceals another.

You knew this already. Try to be patient.
I have no religion really, just a scalp-lock for
good luck and a handful of beads.
They come to me needing, they come on their knees.
They come with devotion, they come for me.

All the animals in the forest, all the birds are
weeping. I alone can hear them – I have not been spared
those powers. Yet look – you cry too. Read a book,
get some work to do.

I will put on more rags, I will paint my face
for you. Orange, grey, royal blue. One bulging,
black false eye. I will smile on the world that waves,
a brittle flower on a blind stalk.

Look up at the stars, those elements of
augury. This child would be born wanting –
sweet shock for his indigent father. See, I have
three fingers and each one honed to a murderous art.
Relax, please, this is no place for moral prudery.

A weak stomach, perhaps?
Or blood is not a strong point in your personal
constitution? It is the death of yourself you must
fathom, not the depth. Do not give in to guilt, try.
Oh this self-effacing ceremony!

That painting there – it is my most memorable
possession. A gift for pathos, you might say,
my licence to practise. See, the woman visits the
grave of her child by moonlight. The diffused light
helps to set it off, don't you think – obscures the
sentiment.

So move from the bed. I must know your face.
Come let us not be ungracious to that audience which has
long entertained me. By that I mean you are one of
many. You insist on knowing? *As many as can dance on the
point of a needle*. Frivolous, you must think me, but
it was your choice. No doubt this is what *she* is
thinking – that woman in the picture.

I should be more generous. Take my hand –
yes it is fragile and unshakable, not what you expected.
Look in the mirror; everything is waving. *Goodbye, goodbye.*
Every habit, every gift, every hesitant drift.
Look up at the sky. Somebody is waiting.

Currant bread, simnel-cake and
coloured eggs were eaten on the
picnic. Oh, it was a good
picnic, an elegant one.

We spread the ground with food
for the beautiful women.
Elisa and Mary were joined together
at the hip and shoulder – they were
born that way – joined – but we decided
to let them come on our picnic.

I would not want to be born joined

promise me I will not be born joined to anyone.

WITHOUT TITLE

I wanted to write
a kind of a love poem

simply to say this:

that nothing is simple,
not even holding you now

lying together, lost on the
same bed,

the whole world inside us
an unborn child

that has no father
or mother.

SLEEPING TOGETHER

In my dream you have become
a fisherman. You are going fishing
in my sleep.
"Sharks come to light and blood,"
you whisper, as if you have always been
a fisherman. A shark surfaces beside me;
still I cannot stop dreaming.

In your dream I am a bird,
I am trapped inside your house.
I flap my wings, beat on the windows.
"My house has no roof," you say.
Still I cannot get out.

You touch me, very gently.
You want to make me happy.
You say so, over and over.
You want me to stop dreaming.

In your dream I am dead.
You have made sure of that.
Still I am stronger than you
and more confident.
My hand does not tremble as yours does
when you twist, again, the knife.

In my dream you have become an
undertaker. You are siphoning my blood
under a cold light.
"Sharks come to light and blood,"
you whisper, as if you have always been
an undertaker. Still I go on dreaming.

You touch me, very gently.
You want me to make you happy.
You want me to stop dreaming.
You say so, over and over.

A shark is swimming towards us;
still, we sleep.
"Stop dreaming," you whisper; he surfaces
beside me.
"Stop dreaming," you shiver; he nudges your
blind windows. The shark has become a bird,
like me. Trapped inside your house we are
flying, flying.

"My house has no roof," you cry,
but the shark, too, is dreaming.
Like me, he does not want to stop dreaming.
He does not want to stop dreaming.

BREAK-UP

For David Arnason

All your life he has
lived in you, the
ice-fish. He has fed on
edges, on extremities.
All your life you have been an
ice-fisherman. Frozen and
hungry you are finally breaking.

You count the lonely minutes.
You count the hours.
Your heart beats against the breaking,
rages against the beating.

Your gentle hands are nets,
are knives. Your eyes remember a time
before the ice shifted.

Break a hole in the ice,
let the fish breathe.
Break a hole in your heart,
let the heart feed.

EVEN IN THE ORDERED WORLD

Always the men I love
return to the mountains.
Always they return
to their mountain women.

Always they carry
my tired smell in their hands,
my taste on their shaky fingers.
Only my innocence
ever remains constant.

Always the men I know
love cages. Their women have
sensitive claws and teeth.
At feeding time their habits are
horrible. They pick at the
red mess thinking it is meat.

I do not believe there is a place for me
in those mountains, or a cage that could
leave me lonely enough to enter.

Even in the ordered world
choices become difficult.
The men I will never stop to love
have lives that deserve
some miracle.

When I first came to the river
I was afraid to cross. It was a
river of ice in a season of ice
and my cold cries echoed like the
tolling of spectral bells.

A woodcutter lived in the woods
beyond the river – I could hear
his ghostly song. He was carving
a woman, an offering to the river-
god. She was an angel of mystery,
all witchery.

It was the winter solstice, the
sacrifice. I filled up my shoes
with ice. I filled up my warm body
with ice. Even the black dogs of
Odin with their jaws dripping fire,
even the oyster-fattened cats with
their claws gripping – and my gripped
heart; everything was frozen.

The old man came down to the river,
the woodcutter. His eye was like
snakebite, my skin milkwhite. He
took my hand, shivering as it was,
and the river cracked. There were
white bears under the ice who woke
and he spoke to them.

They were curious. They rose like
apparitions from their coffins lined
with snow. They nodded their white
heads like white weathervanes though
there was no wind.

They were messengers from the dead –
the old man led me out across the ice.
On the far shore waited the river-god;
he was expecting someone. I told him
I had no reason to go on, no reason
to turn back either.

The ice was melting – the whole world
thawing and shifting. Even my body
warmed, my witch-heart warmed to his
cool offering. The waters were rising
but we sat casting pebbles like bored
anglers.

More mysterious than angels, river-god,
woodcutter, and I sat watching the white
bears. They were fleeing to higher
ground, wading inland as the world
ended. Three survivors with no future
we sat uncaring as the world ended –

as if there were anywhere we could go.

SEA CHANGE

Off shore
the fish thread
like lures through the
waterweed.
We don't
know each other.

A lunar wraith,
the moon rose for me.
I regretted the
dark sea,
the wreathed birds
riding outward on the wind.

I've watched birds
before this
on other beaches –
I've seen the tide
make a ghost of the moon.

I gave the world up:
the sea claimed me.
Half fish I breathed
in uncertain water.

I trusted no one,
living again
in the cool depth of
mirrors, turning against fate
in the windy gulfs.

I needed to
touch you, to feel
a fixed skin. My eyes stopped
at stone, closed like a
drowned man.

It was
only beginning.
Half blinded I came
wrecked out of the
sea, no fish at all
but weathered and cold.

You were there
to meet me. Each day
you concealed more, knew
less of me. My eyes fed
and became strong.

I had you then.
No doubt all journeys
end this way,
drifting inland under
a dry moon, regardless
of tides.

ONE-SIDED WOMAN

I

Her heart is a bone
laced by the
moon's pull –

for seven days
and seven nights
she is
his hunger.

On one hand
she wears a ring,
in the other she
holds a knife.
Her tongue understands
no language,
her face is
not beautiful.

II

She knew by
drowning
she could not avoid the
past –

water filled her
silence
like an old scar
hoarding its own
depth.

III

Between her legs is
the slash of an
underworld –

bracken lips unfurling
shy to the
moss-folds.

One hopes
she is gentle
to rhythms of the
sea.

IV

The flowers she picked
and brought to him
died before she
got there –

her face like a
gargoyle on a
picnic
breaking open
more eggs
than were ever meant
to be eaten.

V

For five months
she paced the winter,
dark with advancing power.

Her breasts
hung like greed
to the shell of her
heat –

her eyes saw
out of habit

her body outgrowing
its own sorrow.

VI

The person inside her
is beating the
damp walls –
knocking on stone
now and again
in the wreckage of
her dreams.

She is
wild-bitten and her
skull rattles.
She does not want to play
like other children.

VII

She is tired
of weedy places,
of thin voices in a
house with too many
rooms.

She imagines a
journey
out to the islands –

trailing a vague
hand, floating
for the shark's sake.

VIII

She knows
the moth's oblivion
in a dry month.

She reads maps
of places she might
like to go

but never goes
anywhere
so many times.

IX

She remembered the time
when three men had
followed her home –

like wolves
in a cold winter,
her scent making
its own silence.

X

She will not wake
early.
The bed sleeps with
limbs like
coffin-wood.

She dreams of
caged animals
in an empty
field –

the blank hooding
of eyes
like spyholes to a
slaughterhouse.

XI

After the rain
she went out
quietly

watching
the grey cat
from the
calm centre of a
different storm.

XII

All the men
soon tired of
talking –

she moved to
another room.

Each man drank
in her name
to their dryness –

her eyes like stones
that water
could not reach.

EQUINOX

Sometimes under the night
I hear whales
trapped at the
sand edges
breathing their
dead sound.

I go out into the rain
and see,
my face
wrinkled like
moonlight
and long nights hard
under the wind's eye.

The stones lie
closer than water,
floating from darkness
like separate tides
to the same sea.

I watch you
with your shadow
come down over the sand:
your knife is
glutted,
your cold hand
has drawn blood out of
fire.
I hear whales
pressing the blind
shore, netted
till I wake binding
weed with water –

how long were you
pinned down
unable to reach
or split the sound?

I hear whales ringing bells
invisible as silence

I hear whales with birds' tongues
and slippery arctic eyes.

How long
did you look

before their eyes knew you?

Do you remember
the colour of their blood?

YATZA

I'd say that
seaweed is where
you came from:
long green
waterweed
person, kelp-brother
to the codfish
turned
belly-up.

I'd say your grandfathers
were birds
who flew out of
darkness.
Their bones mark
the channel now –
you can see them if you wait
for low water.

I'd say your father was an
eagle – chipped a raven
out of stone. She
was your mother.
Your sisters scuttled like
giant crabs from her
womb, but you swam
like an otter from the
sea-egg that was
you.

Black-eyed,
scaly, darker than
the rest – she knew
water was your
element. Each day

the tides shift but you are
calm and unchangeable.

Someday they'll
bury you
all wrapped in
cedar-bark – sea-warped
and tangled with the
weed. You'll
sink like a
bone to a
similar fate,
your hair wound up
and your eyes tight.

I'd say they'll wait
for you, for the
beak of the night to
open. They'll hear your
voice on the
turning tide.

I'd say you'd surface
when the moon was
new, rising
like a whale out of
nowhere
and then sounding
the closed waters.

FISHING ON A SNOWY EVENING

How close you come
to being alone.
How close you come
to needing no one.

River is silent, silver
over stone. You are a link
between air and water.

You are alive.
You cast your line out
into the cool shallows;
river rises into shadow
secret and heavy.

A fish jumps.
River ripples and bends –
how close you come
to your own reflection.
Your body surfaces and breaks –
how close you come
to perfection.

Snow falls from the cold
sky, snow covers your closed
eyes. It drifts into your
deep tracks, over the way you
came, over the way back.

How close you come
to innocence at this moment,
how close you come to emptiness.

Snow falls down
out of the cold sky.
It fills your narrowing hours.

MACKENZIE RIVER, NORTH

Filled with darkness
we are already late for this river.
Shadows file behind us
seeping into the light of our eyes.
The river is blind
and refuses to stay.
We move past in our silence,
a long black mile,
cast into some huge emptiness
like continents of tooth and stone.

The river is not our only hunter.
White against the road
the slow rain drives us back
against the ground.
Wolves smell us out of our bones,
fish grow bored and swim away.
There is nothing about for us
but fear

        And moving,
        always moving,
        out of the night
        it comes.

**FOR CHARLIE BEAULIEU IN YELLOWKNIFE
WHO TOLD ME GO BACK TO THE SOUTH AND WRITE
ANOTHER POEM ABOUT INDIANS**

Afterwards when we climbed out into the
black hills like two small outlaws determined
to live, the smile on your face provided no
camouflage.

You showed me the village where your mother had
lived, a glint on the horizon like a mirror
tilted in sunlight to guide you safely back.
Not your own mother, you told me, but
an adopted one. They killed her with cheap wine and
took off without paying anything.

Your father was hunting. When he came home
her face was fat as a beer barrel.
He cut off her head and buried it in a sack.
The police claimed the rest of the body.

Later while you gathered food, I picked flowers.
The foxtails and the fireweed made a perfect bed.
I did not ask for words this time, or forgiveness,
or even a dream to help me sleep.

That morning I had seen you shoot an arrow
three miles over the lake. Whatever you hit
died. Together we rowed out as if
some bond had been made; all day I grew stiff
under your bright shadow.

That night I was cold when your quick fingers
cut into me, picking the choice bits.
There was no way to stop the bleeding then,
or the stench of my last supper. You wrapped
each piece carefully, my heart among them.
Thirteen red bundles. You laughed as I counted.

You made me whole at last. I was breathing lightly
though you held up my lungs as if to prove I was
only pretending. Blood spilled over my face, onto
my pale hands. My eyes had filled up
with something we would call tears but
weeping, you told me, was part of another ritual.

Then you put price tags on all my bones,
souvenirs for summer trade.
I understood then that I did not own anything,
not even the past though there were some crimes
I could not deny easily.

I wanted to make peace but you said
there were no survivors. You spat on your
skinning knife, beginning to make progress.

SKOOKUMCHUK

For Tom York

I guess it's in
my blood
to want to be like
Emily Carr. I don't know
much about her
but we've been to
some of the same
places.

The north is
the end for me –
I'm in love with a
man I'll never
meet.
Indian Jimmy from
Nanootkish (was there ever
such a place?).

Emily and I
shared him for a while –
I know that. He was
impossible to paint
and what's more
she found the forest
a deeper attraction.

*The eagle
eats the land*,
I write in my
journal. A nurse
wraps my wrists and
says next time
don't use
third-rate machinery.

Give me back
my own:
I want to go where
Ninstints found his
name.
Jimmy rows
further into the
sea-drift
Emily says
it's too rough
to go sailing.

She paints
the unexposed skin,
the masks behind
loss. My notebooks
have been empty
up until now;
I write often to
Nanootkish
but my letters
always
come back.

AT NOOTKA SOUND

Along the river
trees are stranded
bare as witches
and dark as the woman
who never learned to love one man.

(In the north
a woman can learn
to live with too much sadness.
Finding *anything* could be hard.)

The river is haunted
with the slippery black eyes
of drowned pika –
you fish for something quite improbable
expecting those thin dead eyes
to begin to see.

Sometimes along the way
the water cracks
and Indians must mend the river
after every other net –
men with fat dog's eyes
and humps
who cast themselves
towards fish in stone.

What could only be one lifetime
(who can go on pretending forever?)
is when the ground turns cold
and the night is so still
you can't remember having anything to hear.
You lose yourself
and off into the distance
the last birds are throbbing
black and enormous
down towards the sea.

AGAINST

kuganaa . . . black magic . . .
rats inside . . .

Up past the Indian graveyard
the sea has
uprooted trees.
The dead dream of
nets flashing,
clutch against
kuganaa –
dark magic in a
dying tongue.

I dig for a
darker stone,
the kind
rats are afraid of.
Black and silvery
to keep out evil,
I pick away the
mirror-flakes
to hold against
kuganaa.

The beach scuttles
from under me,
drags its
shell-hoard from the
strain of tides.
I hear rats
waking in the
graveyard,
growing fat by the
memorial.
Rats giving birth
under the long grass.

I cross the old bridge
by daylight
avoiding their eyes.
I move
without seeing
into the tall cedars,
far past the
dead flowers.

I slip like a memory
following the dark
road

my white skin has
fooled them
every time.

REQUIEM FOR TALUNKWAN ISLAND

*Talunkwan Island, named after the Haida word
for phosphorus, lies in the South Moresby group
of the Queen Charlotte Islands. In recent years
clear-cut logging on the steep slopes of this
island has caused massive erosion and landslides,
and has made reforestation impossible.*

I
"You need not think they will make such a continual
noise of singing in Skedans Creek as they used to
in your previous existence."

HAIDA MOURNING SONG

The sad ghost of a
dead art I come
down out of the mountains.
I am weak with hunger
and my hands, oh like the
cedar trees, are stumps.

The animal inside me
sniffs the breeze.
It is all lonely darkness
breathing in and out like the
sea. Over the slick rocks at the
lip of the falls I fell
back through my father's words
and into the womb of my mother.

I almost feel whole again
remembering how it was.
I could move among the trees,
embrace heaven and rock when
gods dwelt in all places and
everything was singing.

I was raven, eagle –
I flew up up up into the top

of the salmonberry bushes.
The sky was a wilder place
in those days, wider and cleaner.
I recall you could travel
just singing and flying,
with the sea all phosphorus
lighting the way below.

Now I sit and stare at
the ocean. Sometimes for days I sit
and watch. Who hears the songs
when the voices are silent;
who remembers the great sound we used
to make, on the shores of an island
we thought would last forever?

II
"What do they think they will attain by their ships
that death has not already given them?"
                    WILLIAM CARLOS WILLIAMS

The submerged rocks sleeping like
whales did not stop them,
nor the winds that beached our
canoes and sent the
kelp gulls crying inland.
We thought their sails were clouds,
and how could we have known better.
The sky was overcast and black;
my old grandmother picked cloudberries
and hid them under her hat.

The ships had come to trade –
what wealth we had was little then,
and nothing now.
My mother had to go begging
that winter. A young girl she grew
quieter and older.

If my hands were good I would
carve her something – the moon
gripped in a raven's beak –

but where would I find wood enough,
or the right spirit.
I lit a fire instead and stood in the
coals. A ship sailed out and
darkness tossed the sleepers from
its hold.

I felt tears on my young face
like rain down a mountain rock.
Something was lost; I could feel it
as I followed a deertrail to the
seacoast.

It was a day's journey
but it took me all my life.
At the end I found a highway and
people living in houses.
The trees were cut down and the
land had been sold for a pittance.
The old names were gone and the
ravens, for once, were silent.

I took the eyes of an owl
and stitched them into my head.
I took the wishbone of a foetus
and pressed it into my breast.
I sailed up into the clouds and
blackened the sky with earth.
The sky would mourn too, the way
death does, in the roots.

III
"But they could die for years, for decades,
so tall their silence, and tell you nothing."
                    HOWARD NEMEROV

They were sacred.
Their silence was something we
lived by, not the noise of machinery
stripping the thickets.

The trees were our spirits;

they have gone into nothingness.
They have become mortal, like us;
we diminished them and they have become
human.

Eternal life is unlivable
yet men rut like fat bucks in the
bush and women go on sighing.
It's a sad thing to be lonely in the
body, but to have no body at all –
that's the loneliest.

If I had the penis bone of a bear
I would point it at that woman.
Now there are no trees left to
shelter us, and the grass where we
could have lain is withered and
unyielding.

I wish there could be forests upon
the earth again, a place for our
children to gather. I wish the trees
would return during our own lifetime,
take hold and grow that we might
live again under their silence.

Now men talk of the wood they must
carry, they speak of the weight in
tired voices. I remember a time
when the whole world was singing,
and a love that kept us bound
by things we could not know.

IV
"The wind blows where it will, and you
hear the sound of it, but you do not know
whence it comes or whither it goes; so it is
with every one who is born of the Spirit."
JOHN 3:8

They took my hands
and threw them into the ocean.

I saw them scuttle towards Skidegate
like white crabs with supernatural power.

It is sometimes necessary to sit
and say nothing,
to watch what takes shape, and
changes, out of that silence.
It is sometimes a necessary violence.

They left my skull; I suppose
it told them nothing. My eyes had seen
the rivers full of fish but now the eyes
were older and, like the rivers, empty.
The salmon have gone elsewhere to find
their origins. Like the ghosts of my
people, they have no country.

In my chest there is something that
hurts. It once was a heart
but now it's a hole and their
fingers are eager to probe it.
I cannot tell them how life is when the
soul has left it; the body does not die
but how can they know that.

They do not remember why they were born.
They only hope to find mercy.

I WANT TO REMEMBER DAVID

I want to live on the same island
as David

I want to drive down to 'Charlotte
in his '56 Buick Special
stopping along the way to pick mint
at Miller Creek and briefly
at Jungle Beach for lamb's quarters

if they're in season

I want to wait at the Landing
while David gets the clock-radio going
and leaves the car on display at
Skidegate Esso
where neither the highest nor
any offer shall necessarily
be accepted.

I'll bring armloads of lilac from the
condemned house where we stayed once

I remember there was that
grand occasion when David did a dance,
a striptease for the Mounties who came to
search everyone:

David was a real shocker in
black pumps.

I want to remember David
drifting in a leaky skiff without oars

alone in the rain at the north end of the world
with a picnic basket full of love letters
from Christopher.

is soul-travelling on the
Tlell River
spirit-dancing up the clam-banks
looking for trouble.

Josef's ghost is reading
The Anatomy of Melancholy
mumbling about atrocities
swigging a Skidegate Cocktail.

Josef's ghost goes hunting with a six-pack,
picnics beside the Geikie under a collapsible
umbrella.

Josef's ghost spooks geese on the
muskeg, sabotages the underground
telephone cables.

Josef's ghost courts
young Janey Brown, leaves wreaths
on her worn front doorstep.

Josef's ghost glows in the dark,
frightens the daylights out of our daft Jamie.

Josef's ghost wears a yellow hardhat,
goes to IWA meetings and
leaves abruptly.
Josef's ghost declares bankruptcy at the
Kaien Consumer's Credit Union.

Josef's grave is a National Monument.
Louie's Harriet gives guided tours on
local holidays.

Josef's grave is cluttered with
old wrecked engines,
it is littered with statements from
used-car dealers.

The last time I saw Josef I was sitting beside
the ditched VW

and Josef hitched a ride into Port to scrounge
spark plugs and a new battery:

he was a real genius.

and Mike Davis just back from his
holiday brings us the bad news.

Jack Miller pours another whiskey.
His old lady has left, moved to
Pouce Coupe. So far *he's* got the kid,
but there's going to be a fight.

Mike feeds the airtight,
Helen cooks the spaghetti.
"*They were wiped out in a car,
I don't know how it happened.*"
Most likely Joanne wasn't wearing her glasses:
they'd just come from the Commune
and Brother Love says glasses are crutches.

I remember you, Vern, at Cape Ball one winter.
We swam naked in the river.
And when the time came for you, Joanne,
you too lay down naked.
Vern delivered your second baby.

Mike says your babies are safe,
they were riding in the back.
Nobody knows how it really happened.
It happened a long way from the Islands.

Helen serves the spaghetti.
That Christmas at Cape Ball we had
smoked salmon, poached that spring.
Vern, you Viking, driving your old
VW over the Cape Ball River at
high tide – you said you'd lost
three of them that way but you
kept on trying. "*A good Volksy will do
300,000 miles on one engine.*" And once,

broken down in the rain, you stopped to
offer me a ride.

Your deaths bring me closer to my own.
Friends die, friends go on living.
I visit the graves of my friends,
the houses of my friends.
Mike says he felt at home in the Commune;
Jack Miller says he hasn't time to
stay for dinner.

I eat my spaghetti, silently.
I think that being alive must not
mean very much.
Between mouthfuls I leaf through
Patrick's postcard collection:
Africa, Victoria, the World Famous
Sea Lion Caves in Oregon.
Some of them I recognize – they are
written in my own handwriting.
The messages are indecipherable now,
the ink already faded.

We talk of this and that.
Jack's latest artifact and the
illegality of eagle feathers in
Idaho.

And Vern and Joanne, dead.
Outside in the stillness a mad dog barks
at his own shadow.
Mike pours the wine and there is some
good cheese for afterwards.

Outside in the trees a dead wind is rising.
We eat our spaghetti, silently.

We are happy to see each other after a
long summer. More whiskey for the glass
and Jack Miller says he may after all
have time, this time, for supper.

DOUBT BEING THE MEASURE OF WORTH

Part of every journey is
not wanting to go on

not wanting to get there,
to take risks   and so on

Marilyn had a moment of doubt
in Nitinat Camp   Wednesday morning
after a long drive in   through
                        Lake Cowichan and
Caycuse ·

        we were going to   Clo-oose
we'd planned it for some time
having come this far

        Michael and I were determined to
keep moving.

We rented a boat from Mike Thompson
he said he would bring us up the
lake after lunch
                    the lake being a bit
choppy

dangerous in fact

    Marilyn said it was
famous for being dangerous and
untied her hiking boots
        just in case.

        In the boat I felt the fine spray
over my neck and face
                        I admit I had a moment
of doubt myself
                        wondering
if the boat was safe.

But out there on the lake I was
happier than I'd ever been before
far away from confusion
                        the kind of happiness
I could trust
                        the kind of happiness
that is not possible.

Nothing existed beyond that moment
beyond the far edges of the lake
        the three of us
                smiling
        the three of us together for the
first time in the boat built by Mike Thompson's
        late father.

Oh my ancestors if you could see me now
        floating and drifting
        alive and dreaming
if you could wake up out of your long sleep
long enough to breathe again this
                                breathing earth
these living rocks   this tide
this   lichen-carrying wind

I would be happy to welcome you
you would be welcome to share my happiness.

When I am old I swear I shall remember this day.
When I am too old to go anywhere I shall
remember sharing an orange with Mike Thompson in
Brown's Cove after we safely landed.

SONGS OF THE SEA-WITCH

Long Beach, Vancouver Island –
Victoria, B.C., May 1969

I

Soon you will be gone
out of my life
forever –
you will put on your shoes
and your coat,
you will say

I am just leaving

that will be all

and I will weep tar
for this love of ours that should have been.

Now it is dark, my love,
O it is dark.
What alternatives do I have
after dark?
I take another lover –
for him I am more alive than others.
I come with half-mad eyes
from the soul of a bird
pounding after him
at early dawn

so mad
and so utterly lost.

Once we dreamed
of the same stone.
He is flawless, at first
so I take –
I have nothing to give
and where I shrink
each dawn from skeletons with
their knees drawn up and

old men with
blood in their hair
it is his eyes
who stagger before me
forcing me down
until I admit to
his miserable pain.

Now it is winter
and I must avoid traps.
Like a whore
I am carefree and I hurt.
Go away, I tell my lover,
I have drowned by natural causes,
my instincts say
there is grace in death.
Go back to your woman,
her mind may be cruel
but her body is warm.
I am hardly alive.
My heart is an old rag.
My bones are not sensational,
they are just there.

I am the last one left
with blood on my hands.
I want to know
where self-destruction ends.
I want to know
how much to believe
so that after you have left me
and the real bond begins

after I have left you
the refusal will be in triumph
and not a loss.

II

I wanted to know
what was happening
then.

I ran to you
waving my arms
and cried

"The mountain is on fire,
the mountain is on fire,
who will stop
the mountain burning!"

But you weren't with me
you were away with
somebody else.
Your mouth was full of
her breast, heaving like scissors
on the outer edges of her skin.

You made me
alive with anger.
I went off
tramping down the river
and made
in the rocks
a bird – I gave it flesh
and a hideous name
and called it you,
sent it flying
where no one else could see
and brought it down
with another stone.
Then I lay on my back
in your blood
as the mountain burned
in the dust and the
wild strawberries
and you,
undisturbed by it all,
went on loving her
instead of coming with me
to watch it burn.

And you did love her,
right into the sand.

I saw you hesitate for a moment
on the brink of her thighs
but then
you drove her down
down and down
tearing your face
for her
on the cold hard sea
and your eyes bled
needing more than anyone could give.

I cried
as the mountain fell to ash
and from ash into stone
but I kept on burning
and being burned
until she divided us
with a final death
and drove you away from me
out of the tide
and into the hands
of the darkening trees.

III

I nearly missed you
altogether
this time –
I was stamping around my knees
in mud
and peered up
over the ledge
to your stone.
There were birds there, my love
and a music box that
sang if I wanted it to –
at first I thought it was
all quite nice
but then I discovered
the shredded bones of people
half-lost in feathers,

people I had hardly known.
I touched a hand and
pulled out the body
of a boy. Pieces of him
had already learned cruelty.
There was a dinner gong
and wind chimes for the wind,
an elaborate setting
for so many dead.

You must have turned quite mad
with the sun.
I thought you were
the prince of this place
but look at you now
watching me from
three forests away,
your eyes as slow and blind as thumbs.
I thought this was
your island,
this palace for the dumb.

You told me
this was your throne
so I came here
and found a tree instead
with branches so smooth
I had to dance all around.

But you can't abandon me here like this
and if you do
I shall decide my own way back.
I am tired of birds
and sick of dancing.
I am half-afraid of you.
The light I am fading with
is a graveyard for lovers –
everything ends here
alone with the cold.

IV

I was not sure
that I believed what he was doing
as he sat there at the window
all winter long with his flashlight
dragging things out of the water
and onto the sand.
He wanted
some relic of the past to reappear,
some wreck on a
visionary reef of gold,
a naked goddess,
the treasure he once made me
knowing I would lose it all.
In his torchlight
he made the birds go dancing,
he called down planes –
all winter long
it was like this,
he never changed.
Only once I dared to creep away
to be alone
and looking back I saw him
shine the light
at his own direction,
crumple his shaving mirror
and stuff a hundred shapeless pieces
down the eye of his horrible throat.
I came back
hoping he wouldn't notice
my broken hands. I cared for him
too well.

Then it was summer
and where he guided in the
ships at night
he shone a false beacon
and was the dangerous rock.
Slumped in his chair
he is bearded now,
he has never moved
but he likes the change.

I am his widow
lost to the autumn and the
spring. I lie alone
and nod to day and night
like kelp,
mistress of his harbour,
keeper of his silent chair.
When this day is over
there will be nothing left for me to do
so I sing in circles
and wade out through memories of his light
not for any lover's eyes.

v

He may come back alive
some time
someday soon
he may come walking
out of the nettles, his boots
astounded with sting,
his long face blistered
from the kiss of a sun-dried girl.

He is my hunter
too.
When we lie down in the trees
I close my eyes to love
but I am never asleep for long.
I am always
watching him, he is nobody's shelter
in any way.

Last time he went from me
too long
to somebody else's ruins
another continent away.
Children ran wild
through his beard, he was not
careful enough, he
didn't remember me.

Is there really this much
desolation
or is it just that
I've found it all?
– Who decides these things
you said
as I crept away
and threw a stone from my shoulder
over the sun.

Next time you leave for the forest
I will be staying here.

VI

Up until now
I felt as though I had been
forever hanging on to something.
I half-loved you,
the empty places took on the shapes
of change, the stone I felt
survived, still as stone
and I lived within you
where the wilderness invaded
destroying the equivalent of days.

But I had forgotten about the city.
Because I loved you
too much
I had marked time
on the spot of our solitude –

"Goodbye –
I will only be leaving for a year"
is now what I know I must say

but who am I fooling
wrapped in the coin of
snake skin, coiled in the
sight that crumbles in
expectation

I swear
I will never be back again.

O alphabet,
you letter-perfect
language! It is difficult
this –
coming down.
In a woman's law
there is no alternative
to sadness.
There is only blackout
beyond her
and no cure for what is
temporary
and lies between.

There you will remain,
angry
at the memory of it all,
unable to penetrate
a similar heart as your own
you will try everything,
even to outlive me
with some amazing or immortal feat.
Finally, in exasperation
I will eat my way out
of my own skinny veins
and unwind in all the labour
of that cruel and last descent.

I will betray you, my lover,
I will ruin you.
I will smash my rotten detestable heart
on all the preoccupation
of your mind.
Not even wounded
I will lie accused for centuries
cold in the slime of the
snake-seraph with his head-dress
and fangs
vomiting up my memory
of you
broken with the murder
of the universe to come.

NIGHT WIND

Somewhere out there
we are animals –
in the cold wind always
blowing from death,
breathing its
storm under my
dry skin,
beating bone-music
into the tight black drum
of my fear.

Wind cast us
in all directions –
my face collapsed
in your eyes,
pieces of your heart
came away in my hands.
I felt some strange cold
distance of touch
in your body I've entered
a hundred times.

Wind gives
no reason for taking,
only tears at the
blind window
as I lie
silent against you.

Against you.
Our bodies know
what the silence is.

The sound has
no ending, like a dream
you never return
to. I still remember
that emptiness –
the first whisper
of darkness and the
dead wind rising
all night.

These are the black woods,
my first asylum. Down at the
river's edge, in my own way
given to the monstrous.

Voices I called to
out of the blind fog
drew me that way.
Into the wet woods
calling them: they do not
answer and I am
possessed again.

*Stay with me – you who are
other to all
I am – you whose darkness is the
shadow of my birth.*

I could not escape it –
they were everything.
Moss grew over their
faces, seaweed was
their hair. Theirs
was the way the
wet sounds as
everything condenses.
Theirs were the still fires,
the moon's frail worth.

*Stay beside me – you I have
returned to
more times ever than
anyone; you I have returned to
other than anyone,
other to myself.*

I shiver. It edges
the unfamiliar; it
lessens me. Dark with the secret
I am hunted under,
theirs are the wounds
beneath the scars.

Voices out of the night
and the fog, voices of the womb
conceiving me. I believe in
creation, in flesh that binds
and is mine without knowledge.

I have forgotten more: I have
lost more than remembrance.
While I slept the voices were
dying – they are dead now and
do not answer.

>   *Stay with me. I need your*
>   *comfort now. One wish is that*
>   *you would return and*
>   *all would be warm again.*

Stay with me. Out on the
trailing edges of darkness
I scatter their last bones before me
to my will.

THE RIGHT WORD

For Sean

I

The silence you
filled me with
is a dream I
cannot remember

nothing
replaces you

not even
the silence.

II

The words
I once spoke for you
have vanished

memories
like caves
are filled with the
dead bones of
things.

Among them
your skeleton
heavy with sleep.

The words
I tried to
wake you with
is the reason
you are smiling.

III

In a dream
you stand over my grave
trying to find the right word
to end the funeral.

It's strange
since I haven't died
and I can't seem to make you
believe that.

You stand
looking uncomfortable
holding my old
umbrella.
I get the feeling
you know how
the dream ended.

IV

When this photograph
was taken
were you thinking about
death?
What thought is frozen
that only begins to thaw
in time and through
constant exposure?

You *look* dead
only your eyes moved
at the last moment.

Maybe you thought
about me.

V

Because the wolves
smell you
your dream won't
save us

it only puts words
between silence
and death.

Your silence
is no answer
until I can hear it

as long as
you pretend to sleep
I won't wake you.

THE WOLF

I killed a
wolf
but I knew
he wasn't
dying.

He spoke to me –
it wasn't you
but the voices
came from you.

I can't remember
the words he used,
if they *were* words
or just wounds
closing.

I laid him down
under the dark trees.
I listened for his
breath.

I was waiting for the sign
that I would
know you by,
watching for the eyes
that say
you remember.

It seemed to me
that the wolf was
smiling

(how can I be sure)

it looked like
the last smile
you gave me

as I walked out of
that forest
and into another story.

ENTRANCE OF THE CELEBRANT

If you could see me,
where I am and where
the forest grows thick and into me;
if you could reach
the darkest centre of myself
and still know the sign of the animal
where it lies apart inside your skin –

then I would say,
that kiss is *my* kiss;
where our lips have touched
were others, and mine are still.

No one forgets
the music of the animal. I've heard
the sound of the old skin cracking
where his heart has become
the heart of something new.
                              If he could see me,
know me, and not forget it was
he who saw me

and that circles tighten and everything
narrows

but that even I am nearing completion,
that everything I have become is something
already gone –

then the dark trees, the sounds
of water across water, of blood
drying still over water –

then his music is the sound of
nobody listening; the animal I carve out
is the shape of darkness, a sound
that nowhere would dare to form.

Animal! Animal!
You are nobody! You cannot be
anyone.

But I had known that
long before your birth.

So you died then? Only the dead
can know. My lips revealed you
and my black heart has eaten the hole.
Black fingers pulled a small black night
from between us. Animal, animal
so small are we

that no one wanting
deserves death more.

THE PACT

I tried to touch you
with my eyes closed
and felt you waver,
uncertain as ice.

I heard
ice-worms
drowning in your
body, multiplying
in dead numbers.

I think of you often
this way in winter,
needing some immeasurable grief
to carry me through
the season.

I think of you
in the forest,
in the deep snow
making tracks that imagine
no betrayer.

I know you.
I *am* the forest;
my deep scent reels
against the dark.
I unfold
like darkness
and you are lost in me.

Once I discovered
a wounded deer.
Convinced of hunger
I ate its heart.

You know
if I found you dying
I would do the same.

THE FLIGHT

You cannot leave me
   he told me
out on a cold mountain,
his lips shrill upon our troubled skin.
You cannot leave me
   – an old wound set in so far
     that it cannot mend –

The triumph is not in
the man himself, nor in the
women among him.
The triumph is the hazard of the man.

Sadness is a fixed thing
   I told him after
on a windy hill of skaters.
Ice flashed from behind his eyes,
there was a stone
   blinding him.

RETURNING TO THE TOWN WHERE
WE USED TO LIVE

I found this photograph.

A woman is reaching towards you.
Your hands seem to meet
where now my own fall uselessly.
Even the air around me is cruel,
and your creaturely eyes
full of a new hunger.

I seem to have been travelling
all my life. Your last letter written
ages ago says nothing has ended.

Returning to the town where
we used to live
I found this photograph.

A woman is leaning towards you.
Your eyes seem to meet where now
I feel only a stranger.
I had wanted to be so much.
I seem to have been travelling forever.

Just yesterday I flew
over the country where you live,
knowing I would never find you,
knowing I never did.

I saw the new moon holding
the old moon in her arms

I wanted to be held
and to hold you like this.

YOU ARE ON A TRAIN

You are on a train coming down
from the mountains, coming closer and
closer; you have been travelling for a
long time.

Nobody is expecting you.
Your cheek against the glass is cold,
is white. A bird lifts up from a winter
tree, flies towards you out of the distance
as your train begins its slow descent into
poisoned farmland.

You are dreaming, you dream you are
sleeping. Where you are coming from is
cold. You do not remember the name of that
country.

I am not expecting you.
I have made up your bed and closed the curtains.
I have hung your picture back in its place,
put on an old dress, arranged my face.
I have filled my body with your silence; still
I am not expecting you.

You are on a train
you are glad to be travelling
happy to be going somewhere finally,
finally arriving.

You have no memory of the past.
You have no expectations.
You are alone on a train coming down
from the mountains, coming closer and
closer, flying towards me out of the distance.

speeding towards light, the night
behind you, the night

inside your rear-view mirror
igniting the whole sky.

Your eyes are ice,
broken glass on the road at night

you are driving towards the moon,
driving alive out of the night sky.

It is my heart that beats in the
moon's breast, my eyes that mirror the
moon's reflection.

I do not want to share her with
anyone. Remember, it is my moon,
my moon.

WHAT DO YOU DO
WHEN THE MOON IS BLUE

and you're drifting towards
Vermilion, Saskatoon.
I'm at the end of the line and
you're just passing through.

It's a wide wide country
wild and wide
and I'm not familiar
with where you've been.
You are always driving
and never arriving

I'm watching the tide roll in.

Where do you go
when the moon is blue
it hardly ever happens

when it happens, it's real.

It's hard to understand,
difficult to feel. Like the
sun and the moon sharing the
same sky, you see

nothing lasts

nothing lives for long

nothing burns forever
in that sky.

CROSSING TO BRENTWOOD ON THE
MILL BAY FERRY – NOVEMBER 4, 1975

Now, for the moment, everything is promised.
It is a calm bright day.
Not even any mist over the trees,
nor ice in the slippery roots.
No sense of urgency.

We are crossing the water.
I hold your hand needing
only that. The bare sea is simple enough
and the clean sky that no longer seems
lonely. Birds circle the boat
full of their good messages.

Last night snow fell on the
mountains. I woke up
shivering and afraid.
I needed to know everything about you.
Suddenly I needed to know
more than what there was.

Today, for the moment, everything is forgotten.
I hold your warm hand as if it were something
I had just found wanting to be held and
you smile back. Later when we talk
ours will be other voices.
Now, crossing the water,
I am certain there is only us.

FLYING THE FLAG OF OURSELVES

because we have no country,
no place to return to other than
our own bodies

because we are alone
and have reached this place
together

because there is no one to
pray for us,
no one to worship.

It is the flag of innocence,
of joy and celebration.
When we look into each other's eyes
it is reflected there –
we see it is the flag of loneliness.

It is a beautiful flag,
it fills up the whole sky.

It is the flag we fly
because we are alive

the flag of our union
you, love, and I.

and out the other side,
pumping like a bitch in heat,
beast with two backs, the
left and right ventricles.

It has to be love
when it goes straight through;
no bone can stop it,
no barb impede its journey.

When it happens you have to bleed,
you want to kiss and hold on

despite all the messy blood
you want to embrace it.

You want it to last forever,
you want to own it.
You want to take love's tiny life
in your hands

and crush it to death before it dies.

THE GOD OF LOVE

On our first night together
there were sirens
and a new moon

and no doubt there were
different people
turning to one another
in different parts of the city.

It didn't matter;
that's why we had each other.

It was more than just enough
but nevertheless something troubled me.
I moved from our bed to the window
where it was bright. The whole world
around me seemed to be on fire.

The air was black
and breathing became difficult.
I knew I had been mistaken:
I saw that fire was much more than
sudden brightness.

Nothing could have been colder,
I had not dreamed of anything so
dark. The people ran about
crying out to the god who created them.
*The sight of their vulnerable bodies made me
feel humble.*

That was when I drew back to touch you,
knowing we could never wake
before the flames reached us.

I saw the moon
burst like a
puffball from the
stabbed body of the
trees. I imagined
the caught animals –
my familiar among them.

No one would be
saved – I remembered
the vacuum below me,
the stick-house city
burning outward towards
water.

I stepped between
logs – drowned the way
a stone does
forgetful of surfaces
unaltered and
falling endlessly.

Then you –
my familiar –
in one disguise
I'm not sure of.
You are so beautiful
I'd always want
to have you near me.

I remembered
fire; the cold slit of your
tongue opened an
old wound. You drew
your kisses in,
buried yourself in a
new armour.

The fire took everything.
I'm more alone now
than ever.

I dreamed your name
over and over
thinking it might bring you
near.

I heard nothing
but the sound of my own
calling

my familiar
my own
close your eyes down
over me.

FIRE-FEAST

That night flew in
as the shape of a bird;
to the foxhole, little friend,
I ran my course.

A warm secret we knew
was comfort then. The quickening
of the year meant danger.

The first month you stayed
beside me, all gentleness then
without wounds. Under the
cold slopes our blood ran
for safety; in the thickets
they hunted for slaughter.

Then you were a ghost
to me, little and
ruined when you broke from the
moon's heat and ran to earth
in the lost light.
              They made fire
to your madness and
drew you out, careless of the
wood's green for all that death
soon won.

Don't betray me.
Bloodless the thorn will survive
where they danced for nine lives
on the ashes of the feast but
fallen and unmated I will have
no one. To the fire's edge
I trusted them but now I follow
my own footprints back.
                        Crouched
in the dull passage I remember how
I saw you, already running
far in the unfamiliar dark.

All night the
deep bird inside me
circles the
gripped skin. At times
in the cold light
he edges fire.

Beyond him there is
darkness. We know
the mark. Bird of
the bone of which
we are naked, bird of
the black flesh
driven into night.

He comes out of
nowhere, invisible as
loss. Dry as a shadow
his old seed split
from a corpse's heart.

He is black
inside me
circling into life.
I remember that
one night
when all, when everywhere
memory fails.

There is still time.
Our fingers loosen the
earth. Sinking back
into the green fold,
out of the earth's lock
tightening still.

I was falling
even then. That world
edges this wound, that bird
did not choose.

He was
part of us. He fed
in the
moth-light and now
you sleep.

He is part of us.

Now I remember
a dark stone
where you were
sleeping

trailing blood,
trailing blood.

BURIAL OF THE DOG

He would not lie uncovered
for long,
the cracked grave-boards
released his gnawing dust.

His face had
not appeared
though out of the
cramped earth
one eye had shed
for all to see.

His fur was worn –
an unsexed carpet ploughed
where time and light passed like
relics of an ancient crime.

The earth dwarfed him –
knowing this he came
to his own burial.
He unlearned every trick
he made – lay down
like black dawn
on all horizons.

But did not change.
Last winter we found him
unburied once more by rain,
half-running to
recover sleep, tunnelling
through age.

We with our faces closed
saw nothing –
knew the cold memory
stiffened as it dried.
We left him in the
half-light, our footsteps
sly as blood.
Our fear went out to him
from eyes of
other animals.

DOG STAR

I do not remember
the night; that night
I had no way with him.

I was the dog child
follower of stars.
I was the dark one's
brindled stray.

That night the night
entered him –
I left him there.
Uphill where the hawk lives
I carried his bones to earth.

Dog child he whispered,
he was nearest to me then.
I came and the wind
covered us – we lay alone
in sleep.

But rising out of that
dark hill, the shadow
of our last flight fell,
not caring
how the stars shone or
knowing the dust of that
final light.

This was the first night,
dream I remember:
*two wreaths of the
old gods
were fire and blood.*
That was the last time
I followed him again.

Dog child he called me,
I turned to leave.
Stars hung
like chains on my sleep,
moonlight
barred the way.

Sometimes an old man
crouches at the river –
sometimes he is someone
whose bones are not formed.

Sometimes an old woman
with fisher-skin quiver,
sometimes on the low bank
is hungry after blood.

First Man wrenched a
forked tree, spit
the bone. First Woman
was a warm pelt
to carry him into the ground.

"People don't tell out
about these things;
they keep them
down here in the body."
Be careful
of the wolf's cry – he knows
those ways well. Open
the toad's belly and you will
find him there.

"The bone at the back
of the head is best,
a tongue black and swollen
from skin whorls picked
at night." First Woman
was a night cat
prowling the red ant hills.
First Man was
victim, sometimes
a grey fox.

Sometimes an old man
whispers down the smoke-hole,
sometimes an old woman
furrows in the wind.
My skin is thick
with the dark seed
of their coming –
the blade of a fine axe
wedged between my eyes.

FINDING LOVE

The thin smoke stings my eyes;
my fingers, like bees, in search of you.
It is doubtful, coming here by night,
that I shall return by you
in the same shape as I came.
We look alike, sometimes,
lying side by side; love's own posture
but all an empty stake.

I waver like a child
having fled the sea. It is not
what I expected, the dark fires,
the sullen turn of ground. Everything
must learn how *I* have dreamed it:
a misshapen thought, or else,
a darkness forever without a name.

From my bed I could hear
the ripe wound open, the thick sea
pouring in. I told you then
the first lie I had in my heart;
the carcass of a dull animal
slipped between our sights.

REFUSAL

These are not all lovers,
these half-shapes.
When they reach for each other
their teeth leave marks,
they spend
in each other's blood
something beyond love.

They are insects,
and what is worse
they are insects that feed upon
their own decay.
They have pursed reality
from some
worn-out maggot hell
and there is
no saving them,
there is
no yesterday
when they come down.

One day, all suddenly over,
they find themselves alone. The rocks,
for a change,
have worn down the waves.
There is
danger in sanity
there is danger
in sanity
there is danger
in not understanding loss.

AFTER THE BATTLE

Unaware that anything was wrong
I crawled out from under you
after the battle
and stood
remote and changed
in the place beside you
that should have been your own.

Yours was the only corpse, I noticed.
Some small animal
circled cautiously behind your eyes.
Your mouth had no edges,
no place for hanging on.
It was, instead, a place for lizards.

Your body is the sanctuary
for all the wildlife
that isn't me. A remnant of your hand
encloses all.
I am some bad flower
sent deliberately to spoil your grave.
I grow best in blood.

Lying here,
you accuse me in the darkness
without even turning
certain beauty to design.
You want everything to reappear
out of a past I can't explain.

I am not at fault
because you fell in a place of stone.
The blood will dry,
the stone will still be cold.
Your body will be
the singular thing
containing all.
That is –
           nothing to remain,
           nothing to destroy.

CELEBRATION

Being somebody's last woman
and the only passenger of the day
I rode out after madness,
that long journey beginning nowhere
meeting shyly at motels
not for each night's love,
but sliding around the edges
from earth to earth
on parts of a face
that love wore out.

Of course I'm still living.
No one has taken too much blood
although I admit I stole some extra
where fine needles had coffered
bundles and rolls of it. I came back
after to burn the hospital down.

But no one will find me here
asleep in my bones as polished as the night.
I am bled now
like the end of a spear
and blunt as a carpet
ruined once by careless feet.

One day the right disguise
will work, the right frame
slide into place
like counted medicine.
One day I may give up everything
and wear that disguise
to its final sleep.

Today there is
damage being done.
Damage unrewarded in the
history books of the law.

Damage being done to the
children, waking in the
too-bright sun.
Damage being done to the
eloquent, the lascivious.

Damage is being done to the
ordinary, to the invalids
in their frail carriages.

Damage is being done to the
whole world, to all the
nodding, careering people.
They are bandaging one another,
bandaging the damage.

Even the artists with their
crude tools, or doctors
with their cool instruments –
even the undertakers,
they cannot stop the damage.

I flutter my tiny hands,
useless, useless.
I undo my dress,
it is useless, useless.
I see weapons twitching in
grisly fingers.
It is useless, useless.
I smell blood and guts and begin
to feel generous.

Damage is being done to everyone.
It keeps us nasty.

GRAVE-DIRT

One god
distributes the light.
By error on that day
he descends to hell.

Hell is just an impression

luck-balls from the
death-owl's mask.

Raven unsheathes his
beak-knife,
his voice is made of
glass.

Woodpecker is the
hero,
his bad luck is
crossed.

His words are
the colour of mutiny

mumbling about birth
in different dialects

never seen on Fridays
because on that day
he returns to hell.

A clerical error
a conjurer
a death.

Woodpecker is
turned upon
picking among bones:
the eagles, the
long songs,
are bad for the memory.

There in her black skirt hides
the skin of a deer,
the flesh under the shape pulled taut
to hide no other reasons
than her own.

I am this shape
               of *this* woman or
these five women tugging at rags,
tossing the twisted
animal skin inside them,
pulling me always from the centre
out.

I am this shape of this animal
the skin does not change
but is tossed in the shape of a man.
These five women
retrieve him, let loose their skin
set aside their skirts

and the man crawls in among them
as anybody else's death.

He arrives just the same
from the wrong direction. Reduction,
a funeral style, the man says, smiling
as the skin burns away in confusion.

Their small lives
are his idea
also.

GENESIS

He could not rest
until there was water,
finding his words hard –
blue nuggets at the
lip's edge.

He dreamed of water.
Once a drop fell
in the bare light
and the fire eased.
He licked it up.

Scrawling across his belly
a tense yellow blank,
he woke up finding the earth
dry, covered with small dead
frogs.

THE IMPSTONE

For Roy Kiyooka and Daphne Marlatt

I

The day the man
stumbled and
cursed the stone's
existence

the stone created
woman
out of another stone.

Darkness fell
like a thick velvet
curtain over the
land. The stone saw
that it was good.

And on the seventh day
he rested.

II

This stone has been
rained on
this stone has been
left out in the
dark.
This stone has been
stepped on
though it never hurt
anyone.

Pick up the stone –
you will notice these
scars.
Drop it again
it won't blame you.

III

This stone
is the guilt
each person takes
upon him;

this stone
is a
mass-murderer,
a poet,
a thief.

This stone is a
god, a
failure, a
government.

This stone
stands for
nothing –
it has
no country.

IV

This stone
was an island
once:
tourists would take
picnics to its
beaches;
fishermen would take
shelter in its
coves.

The stone knew
what it felt like
to be sinking.
Some people
changed the
island's name
in memory of a
dead politician.

V

In your house
nobody mentions
this stone.
It is asleep
beside the fireplace,
it is dreaming
of warmth.

Nobody mentions it
because they are
frightened.
Nobody feels it
because they are
cold.

One night
it changes
into an apparition.

Nobody knows why.

Your house trembles
like an animal dying.
It sees its reflection
for the first time.

VI

This stone
knows what it's like
to be chipped away
into nothing
to be blown up
into pieces
to make roads for people
to walk down
complaining all the
way.

This stone should have been
a writer
knowing the truth's disguised
as a bulldozer or a
typewriter

knowing the devil is
always present
wearing a
white carnation

being sucked like a
cigar

until he succeeds.

VII

This stone is
everybody's
culture hero.
He has been made to
explain his dream
once too often.

His dream
is the same scene
over and over.
He is standing with a
loaded gun in his
mouth
trying to explain
his feelings.

DAY OF RECKONING

For David

This morning
the horizon was not
there; I saw a
forest shrivelled
where you had slept
with your twigs of
memory, dry
leaves.

There was no movement,
only the ghost of a
shadow too dead for
seeing
and you
struggling like a
crowded room to
recover silence.

Your mirror-world reflects
your own darkness:
how am I to see?
I witness the world's
conscience – let it all
go by. Somehow we survive
like missing people
though who is to say
where the sea is
without water?

Last night
a dream racked your
vision – this morning
you arrived with a new
finality. You were here
before the dawn reached us –
I heard the day crack
like barriers against fate.

I said
let the world contain
its own madness
or else go down.
It is hard to rest,
you told me,
with so many lives in danger.

But are you really
safer than I am
or does caring lead you
nearer to destruction?
                    I heard
voices in the garden
calling for you – people
trampling over the last days
and all things that grow
for no reason.

TWO MINUTES FOR HOOKING

I

You are leaving.

I have just shown you
my collection of
masks.

You kiss me goodbye
but your face is
trembling.

The masks look like
bad imitations of
you

before you became
my lover.

II

You are leaving.

Outside
you play a
trumpet solo
to a herd of
starving cattle.

I can hear you
from my window
where I wait with my
broken xylophone.

Your wife
is an heiress
from an old
military family.

The only
military music

I know
is the kind that they play
at funerals.

III

You are leaving.

My heart feels like
a shivering egg
that some
wild bird
has abandoned.

You like the
image
but it's too much
responsibility.

What do you
expect
on an island
as small as this?

IV

You are leaving.

First we make love
perfecting
habitual patterns.

A photographer
is waiting
at the end of the
bed.

You take her arm
and smile
professionally.

You don't even hear
the applause.

V

You are leaving.

Already I have
forgotten your
smile.

I think you must make
other people
happy

other people whose scars
are still a
mystery.

IT'S HARD TO BE KIND TO A CANNIBAL

You're killing me
I said
still hoping for
second chances.

I love you
you answered
believing in
lost causes.

I'll miss you
I said
still caring about
reasons. The story needs
thickening. Pass
the blood.

It's easy:
you need me
anyway. I feel like a
feast – we have
too much in common.

You ask me for a
quick meal;
I leave early.
It's wrong to die
on a full stomach.

down along the old canal
wearing an ankle-length overcoat
in spite of the heat

sucking sweets By Appointment
To Her Majesty –
the old girl got a good kick
out of that one.

You should have seen her
doing a gang-scuffle outside the
dancehall

or perfuming her body in one of the
lavatories:

she was perfect.

She dressed for the occasion,
a crowbar up her skirt and a
quantity of quicklime.
Hard luck to the whore found dead
in a weedbed

she was queen of the quick throw,
queen of alley ways.

She was beautiful and we
loved her

pock-marked with a pistol
she danced naked over our faces

queen of the underground

it felt good, good, good
to be lying beneath her.

They all loved her,
the tarts and muggers on the
commercial road.
She had a full heart for a
hatchet-man, a kiss for a killer.

You should have seen her
teetering on spikes

a grudge-bearing scullion she was
obvious royalty.

When she danced we came alive,
when she danced she was really living.

There was no dance she couldn't do,
hard and fast in a small lifetime.

A MAN FROM FRANCE

He's a dancer
he makes you wild

he dances the dance of
lonely women

he's a deserter.

I lived with him
he made me smile

that was enough for me
but not enough for those
French ladies.

Bitches, they were brought up
differently.

They wanted a man to marry,
a man to bury.

They didn't want Harry.

JUST LUST

It was
only just

you were chinless
famous
shutters clicked as we
kissed

I saw the photographs afterwards
and I was barely visible.

I don't make a point
of hobnobbing with royalty

it was just lust
I said, I'm a married woman
anyway.

Flustered by my common touch
you fumbled for my knee

the travelling spotlights paused,
you coughed

the orchestra played
God Save the Queen.